A Poet's Guide To Merced

Vol. 1

Steve Baba

Cover design: Steve Baba

Ways to contact the author:
facebook.com/stevebaba
twitter.com/stevenhbaba

First printing, June 2016
Printed in the USA

ISBN: 1532883528
ISBN-13:9781532883521

Table of Contents

Coffee Bandits Café

Coffee Bandits is a café located in downtown Merced. I happened upon it for the first time to meet a fellow artist. The café didn't disappoint and I regard it as the best café in Merced.

1. Best coffee in Merced.

I don't usually order coffee, but here is an exception. The coffee is locally bought and it has a wonderful taste to it. You can order one, two or three coffees and not get sick of it. You can sit down at the many tables and have your laptop or paper and pen ready to write.

2. Atmosphere

I really like the clientele that frequents Coffee Bandits. From business people, artists and writers, to hipsters and students from the various colleges here in Merced, it is never dull here. The music is not too loud and welcoming. You can spend hours writing your novel or poem or short story and be visually and aurally stimulated here. Coffee Bandits has paintings from local artists on its walls. Shabby-chic furniture, and you are all set.

3. Service

Melissa is the owner and she is a joy to be around. She is very friendly and always makes the perfect drink. When I order my hot tea, it is always delicious and made to order. Melissa is an artist and poet as well, so she knows how to run a coffee shop that caters to them.

All in all, a great place to write. Bring your work to Coffee Bandits and you will not be disappointed.

Carnitas Michoacan Merced

Carnitas Michoacan is located in central Merced. It is after the local Handi-Stop. I have been here many times, and I must admit that this restaurant is one of my favorites.

As you enter the restaurant, the first thing you hear are the jingling of bells that emanate into the air from the opening of the door. You enter a well-lighted room. There are about 12 tables with 4 chairs each at each table. There is an open window right near the front of the restaurant to order your food. On the wall, a selection of food to buy. And various sodas. You can sit and relax while listening to Spanish on TV, or you can take out. I usually wait for my food at one of the tables. There isn't much to look out the windows, but the traffic coming and going is good enough for me.

When my order is brought to me I thank the server and dig in. The menu is a typical Mexican fare-burritos, tacos, etc. I always order the tacos. Carnitas with sour cream. I have never seen this place packed, and that's most likely why I always come back to it. The prices are very good and the sodas are crisp and clean.

This place, the TV being the exception, is a good place to write. Though there isn't WiFi available, there is ample room on the tables and the owners are gracious if you decide to stay for an hour or two. I always leave a tip in the jar for the restaurant before I head out.

Multicultural Arts Center

Where else can you write and get inspiration to write? If you thought the Multicultural Arts Center, you are correct. Situated in downtown Merced, this gallery should be on any writer's itinerary.

You enter the gallery, and the first thing that you see is a 30 foot ceiling. Washed all in white. It is breathtaking. There are paintings everywhere. There is a second story, and there are more paintings there. On the first floor, there is a hallway that leads to a rather small room that has local artist's work; The Arbor Gallery. This gallery is peaceful and quiet. I recommend going to the gallery right when it opens or a little after, as you will go undisturbed.

There are a few seats to sit down and write as you gaze at the marvelous paintings. The light is good. I always feel at peace when I come here to commune with art and writing.

17th Street Pub

Located right next to Coffee Bandits is the local watering hole 17th Street Pub. I always like to have a nice beer or two to relax after writing at Coffee Bandits. The clientele are a younger crowd, but it is good for any age above the age to drink. There is a long wood bar that stretches through from front to back, and there are a few tables with chairs. Most of the time there is sports on the TV.

The bartenders are very congenial and more than happy to help you pick out a good lager or micro beer. They only serve beer or wine here. This place is like Coffee Bandits but with alcohol being served instead of coffee.

I like to order the most potent beer and sip from it as I look outside and see the various Mercedians walking by. There is a place outside of the pub to smoke, if that is something you like to do.

Second Time Around Used Books

This is one of two large bookstores in Merced. The other being Barnes and Nobles. I have never seen this establishment busy, but they must sell a lot of books, or they wouldn't be in business. This a well-groomed store, with lots and lots of books. There are various sections throughout the store, and the sales associate is kind and friendly. I could spend hours there.

The only drawback is that you only get credit when you sell your books to them. But that doesn't deter me from going here and loading up on some books that I want to read.

The prices are very good and I dare you to find a better place in Merced for used books.

UC Merced Library

UC Merced is a very clean, nice campus. But I do have to say, their library is world class. I've been here numerous times and it never ceases to amaze me. There are 5 levels and there is always a good seat and table to be had here.

If you go to the upper levels, you can get a nice view of the campus. There is plenty of space. If you enjoy solitude, then you can go into one of the rooms that have cubicles.

It is very quiet here. Just as a library should be. I have never browsed the books in the library myself, but I do know I am very productive when it comes to writing.

Bonus- you can eat and drink here.

J&R Tacos

J&R Tacos is the premier Mexican restaurant in Merced. I have always loved their breakfast burritos, but they serve more than that. Tacos, burritos, soup, all kinds of Mexican fare. The prices are good, and the food delicious.

Oscar Torres, the owner of J&R's, is a very cool person. He also paints and was exhibited by the Multicultural Arts Center. He has a dark beard with a mustache that is curled on the ends. Talking with him always makes me feel positive.

You can order a beer and sit outside if the weather is nice, if not, then indoors is nice as well. The restaurant inside is decorated with tasteful paintings and colors. If you so wish, you can write here, but this place gets busy at times, so you'll have to choose a time when it's not so busy, like after the lunch crowd.

TREE Magazine

TREE Magazine is the local poetry magazine published by Ben St. Clair. It has the best poets in Merced. I have read each issue, and the poet's works gets better and better with each issue.

This magazine is about 20 pages or so, and the cover is a different image/painting/photo each time a new issue comes out.

Ben is a doctoral candidate at UC Merced. He is a poet, a musician and an artist. I've known Ben for 3 years now. We usually get together once a week to write poems. I have also contributed to TREE, as well as helped in the production of the magazine.

You can grab a copy of TREE at Coffee Bandits and other Merced businesses when there is a new issue out. Or read the current and past issues online.

Appendix : Information

Coffee Bandits
309 W. Main St. Merced, CA, 95340

cb@coffeebanditscafe.com
(209) 383-1200
coffeebanditscafe.com

Carnitas Michoacan ⬜
1540 Yosemite Pkwy. Merced, CA 95341
(209) 383-2605

Multicultural Arts Center
645 W. Main St. Merced, CA 95340
(209) 388-1090

www.artsmerced.org

17th Street Pub
315 W. Main St. Merced, CA 95341

17thstreetpub@gmail.com
(209) 354-4449
17thstpub.com

Second Time Around Used Books
524 W. Main St. Merced, CA 95340
(209) 723-9521

UC Merced Library
5200 N. Lake Road, Merced, CA 95343

library@ucmerced.edu
(209) 228-4444
library.ucmerced.edu

J&R Tacos
437 W. Main St. Merced, CA 95340

jandrtacos@jandrtacos.com
(209) 384-2923
jandrtacos.com

TREE Magazine

treepoetry.wordpress.com

Steve Baba is a published poet and writer. He calls Merced his home, and enjoys sipping tea at cafes, eating good food with his friends, and enjoying the cooler weather in the wintertime.